Pearl Harbor: 56 Fascinating Facts For Kids

David Railton

This book is just one of a series of "Fascinating Facts For Kids" books. For more fascinating facts about people, history, animals, and much more please visit:

www.fascinatingfactsforkids.com

Contents

The Road to War...........................1

Planning & Training.................... 4

The Pilots & Planes...................... 6

Expecting an Attack..................... 9

Setting Sail in Secret...................11

The Attack.................................. 13

America at War........................... 18

Assorted Pearl Harbor Facts........23

Illustration Attributions.............. 26

The Road to War

1. In the mid-19th century, after centuries of staying apart from the rest of the world, Japan began trading with other countries. Much of the wealth that trading brought went into building a powerful army and navy, as Japan dreamed of becoming a major world power.

2. To become a major power in the world, Japan needed vast amounts of coal, oil, and other raw materials. Japan is a small nation, and the only way to get the resources it needed was by conquering other countries. In 1937, Japan invaded neighboring China, before setting its sights on other lands in Southeast Asia and the Pacific Ocean.

Southeast Asia

3. Many countries of Southeast Asia and the Pacific were controlled by the United States or European powers, such as Britain and France. By 1939, the European countries were involved in World War Two and the fight against Adolf Hitler's Germany, so only the United States stood in the way of Japan's plans for conquest.

4. In July 1940, Japan boldly invaded French Indochina (present-day Vietnam, Cambodia, and Laos). The American president, Franklin D. Roosevelt, responded by sending the US Pacific Fleet from California to a naval base in the Hawaiian Islands to discourage further Japanese advances.

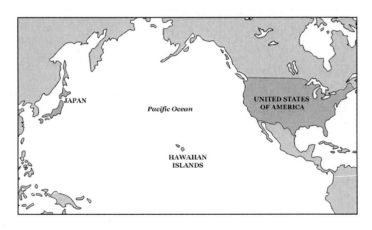

5. The Hawaiian naval base was at Pearl Harbor, on the island of Oahu. It would be the home of nearly 18,000 men and women, eighty-six ships, twenty-three submarines, and nearly 400 aircraft.

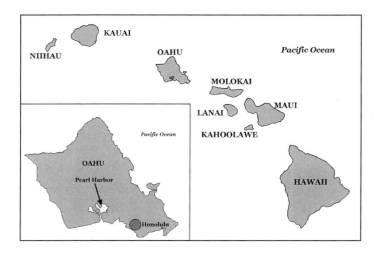

The Hawaiian Islands

6. Japan knew that only the US Navy stood in its way of the conquest of the whole of Southeast Asia. If they could destroy the American fleet then they would be able to invade other countries with ease.

Planning & Training

7. The idea of attacking Pearl Harbor came from the commander of the Japanese Navy, Admiral Isoroku Yamamoto. He knew that the US Navy was very powerful, and that the only way to damage it would be with a surprise attack.

Admiral Yamamoto

8. Battles between navies had always been fought between ships on the open sea, but Admiral Yamamoto came up with the idea of attacking the US fleet at Pearl Harbor by air, catching the Americans completely by surprise.

9. Japanese aircraft carriers carrying hundreds of warplanes would sail secretly to within flying distance of the Hawaiian Islands. Bombers and fighter planes would then fly from their ships toward Pearl Harbor to drop their bombs and torpedoes on the US fleet, before the Americans could start fighting back.

The Japanese aircraft carrier, "Agaki"

10. In the spring of 1941, Japanese fighter pilots began training for their secret mission. They practiced taking off from aircraft carriers, flying low over water, and dropping their bombs onto warship-sized targets. They trained morning, noon, and night for months with hardly a day off.

The Pilots & Planes

11. The Japanese pilots followed an ancient code of warriors called "Bushido." Bushido warriors had to be loyal, courageous, do their duty, and be ready to die for Japan.

12. The pilots tied special scarves around their necks. The symbol of Japan - the "Rising Sun" - and the Japanese word "Hissho" - which means "certain victory" - were sewn onto each scarf.

A Japanese pilot with his scarf

13. Some pilots wore a "Belt of a Thousand Stitches" around their waists. The belts were made by Japanese women, and it was believed that they had special powers to protect against the dangers of battle.

14. Three main types of airplane would be used for the Pearl Harbor attack, each having a different job to do. They were the "Mitsubishi A6M ," the "Aichi D3A" and the "Nakajima B5N ."

15. The Mitsubishi A6M was a one-man fighter plane. It could fly close to the ground and change direction at great speed. It was armed with machine guns in both wings.

The Mitsubishi A6M

16. The Aichi D3A carried bombs under both wings, and one massive bomb on the underside of its body. It could swoop down close to the water to hit its target accurately.

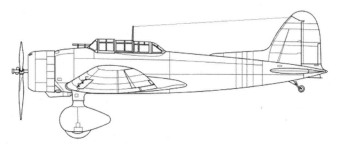

The Aichi D3A

17. The Nakajima B5N dropped powerful bombs toward its target from high in the sky. Some also dropped special torpedoes that had been specially designed for the shallow waters of Pearl Harbor.

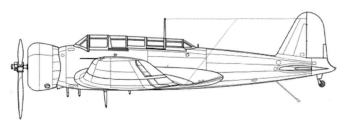

The Nakajima B5N

Expecting an Attack

18. With tension rising between Japan and the United States, some American leaders thought a Japanese attack likely - but not at Pearl Harbor, nearly 4,000 miles (6,400 km) from Japan.

19. Nobody thought that Japanese ships would be able to carry enough fuel for the long journey from Japan to the Hawaiian Islands and back. It was also thought impossible for the Japanese fleet to sail such a huge distance without being discovered.

20. The United States had naval bases in the Philippines and on the island of Guam, much closer to Japan than the Hawaiian Islands. It was thought that one of these two places would be the subject of any Japanese attack rather than Pearl Harbor.

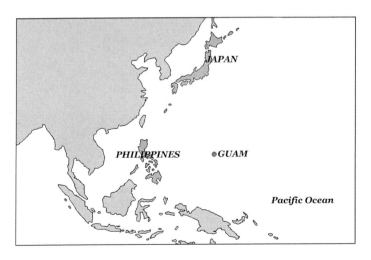

21. The Americans strengthened their defences in the Philippines and Guam. Submarines were also sent to protect other military bases in the Pacific - but Pearl Harbor was left vulnerable and exposed.

Setting Sail in Secret

22. On November 17, 1941, the Japanese fleet set sail. To avoid arousing the suspicions of any American spies, the warships left Japan one by one, each sailing on a different route. The ships eventually met up off the coast of Iturup, a remote island north of Japan.

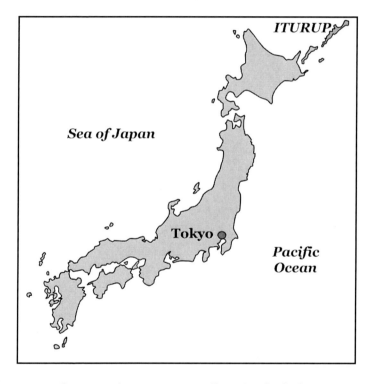

23. The massive Japanese fleet included six aircraft carriers carrying more than 400 warplanes. Battleships, destroyers, cruisers, and submarines would protect the aircraft carriers on the long voyage to the Hawaiian Islands. Eight oil tankers accompanied the fleet so that the ships could refuel at sea.

24. On November 26, the fleet began its long journey to the Hawaiian Islands. To avoid being detected by the Americans, radios were turned off and all sources of light were hidden. The fleet followed a route through the rough, icy seas of the North Pacific to make it unlikely that they would be spotted by other ships.

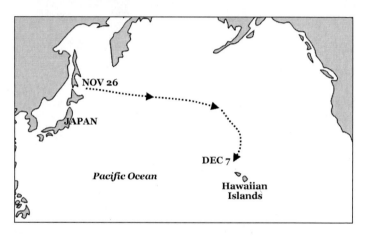

The route to the Hawaiian Islands

25. The Japanese fleet sailed across the Pacific Ocean in secret for ten days and nights. By dawn on December 7, the ships were just 200 miles (320 km) north of the Hawaiian Islands and ready to begin the attack on Pearl Harbor.

The Attack

26. At Pearl Harbor, it was a calm, quiet Sunday morning. Many American sailors were either sleeping late or eating breakfast. Anchored peacefully in the middle of Pearl Harbor were nine battleships, *Arizona, California, Maryland, Nevada, Oklahoma, Pennsylvania, Tennessee, Utah,* and *West Virginia.* These ships would be the main targets for the Japanese.

27. Just after 6.00 a.m. on December 7, airplanes began taking off one by one from the Japanese aircraft carriers. Soon, 183 warplanes were in the air ready to begin the flight to Pearl Harbor.

Japanese planes preparing to take off

28. At 7.55 a.m. the Japanese planes reached Pearl Harbor where more than ninety American ships were anchored. Some of the warplanes flew just fifty feet (15 m) above the water to drop their bombs and torpedoes.

29. Just after 8.00 a.m. the *California* was hit by two torpedoes and a massive bomb. 102 sailors died aboard the battleship and sixty-two were wounded.

The "California" before the attack

30. At 8.05 a.m. the *Oklahoma* was hit by seven torpedoes. Seawater poured in and just eight minutes later the ship had sunk. More than 400 men lost their lives.

31. At 8.10 a.m. a bomb smashed through the deck of the *Arizona* into the ship's ammunition store. In an instant more than 1,000 men were killed. The massive explosion threw the ship out of the water before it broke in two and sank.

Shock waves from the explosion were felt many miles away.

The sinking of the "Arizona"

32. In the first few minutes of the attack on Pearl Harbor, all nine battleships of the US fleet had been hit and hundreds of lives lost.

33. As well as targeting ships, the Japanese also attacked airbases close to Pearl Harbor. Their mission was to destroy American planes before they could get in the air and fight back.

34. At 7.55 a.m. the Japanese began dropping bombs on Hickam Airbase. Hickam was almost defenceless and the Japanese were able to destroy half the planes there, killing 121 men and wounding 274.

American planes at Hickam Airbase

35. At Ewa Airbase, the Japanese used their machine guns to attack. They destroyed all forty-seven planes on the ground, but because machine guns were used rather than bombs there were fewer American casualties. Only two men were killed at Ewa and eleven wounded.

36. The Japanese finally headed back to their aircraft carriers at 8.35 a.m. when all their bombs and torpedoes had been dropped. But twenty minutes later, another attack began with a second wave of 170 planes arriving at Pearl Harbor.

37. The Americans were more prepared for the second attack and were able to fight back with anti-aircraft guns. Most of the twenty-nine

Japanese planes shot down on the day were destroyed during the second attack.

38. The attack on Pearl Harbor lasted less than two hours. Nearly 2,400 Americans were killed and almost 1,200 wounded. Twenty-one ships were sunk or damaged, and more than 300 American aircraft were put out of action.

39. Although the Japanese had won an overwhelming victory, the attack was not a complete success. The most important warships of the US Navy, the aircraft carriers, were not at Pearl Harbor at the time of the attack. They had been safely at sea, and would inflict heavy damage on the Japanese in the months to come.

The American aircraft carrier,
"Yorktown"

America at War

40. The day after the attack, on December 8, America declared war on Japan. Three days later the United States was also at war with Japan's European allies, Germany and Italy, and joined Britain and France in the fight to defeat Adolf Hitler.

41. In the months following Pearl Harbor, Japan was unstoppable in its quest to build an empire in Southeast Asia. Burma, the Philippines, and many more Pacific islands were invaded, and Japan soon controlled more than twenty million square miles (50 million sq km) of territory.

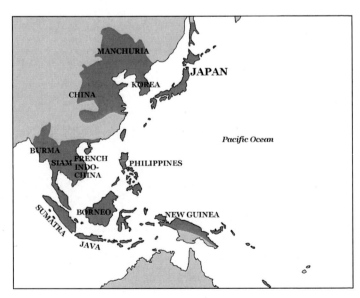

The Japanese Empire in 1942

42. While Japan was expanding its empire, the United States was rebuilding its Navy and repairing the damage done at Pearl Harbor. America would soon be strong enough to take on the Japanese.

43. The turning point of the war against Japan came in June 1942 at the Battle of Midway, 1,200 miles (1,900 km) northeast of Pearl Harbor. Four of the six aircraft carriers from the Pearl Harbor attack were sunk in the battle, and the Americans inflicted a heavy defeat on the Japanese.

American bombers at the Battle of Midway

44. The Battle of Midway brought Japanese expansion to an end, and the US Navy was gradually able to take control of the Pacific and drive the Japanese back to Japan.

45. The war in Europe ended with the defeat of Germany in May 1945, but Japan refused to give in, and the war in the Pacific raged on. By June, the Americans were just 350 miles (560 km) from the Japanese mainland, ready to invade and force Japan to surrender.

46. The Americans had their doubts about invading Japan, fearing the loss of half a million lives - but the United States had another plan to end the war in an instant.

47. For years, American scientists had been developing the most powerful weapon the world had ever seen - the atomic bomb. Following a successful test in the early summer of 1945, where the explosion had sent a plume of smoke 7.5 miles (12 km) into the sky, the bomb could now be used on Japan.

48. The Americans chose the city of Hiroshima as the target for the atomic bomb. It was home to weapons factories, shipyards, and a population of 300,000.

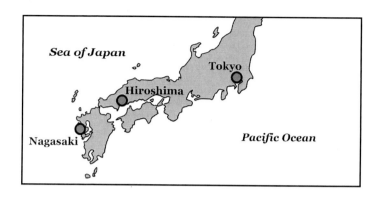

49. At 8.00 a.m. on August 6, 1945, an American bomber flew over Hiroshima and dropped the bomb. 80,000 people were killed instantly and the city was flattened. 80,000 more were to die over the coming weeks from their injuries and radiation poisoning.

The bombing of Hiroshima

50. Three days after Hiroshima, the Japanese still hadn't surrendered and a second atomic bomb was dropped, this time on the city of Nagasaki, with similar results. Five days later, on August 15, 1945, the Japanese finally agreed to surrender. The war with Japan was over at last, but the date of December 7, 1942, would be remembered in America for a very long time.

The bombing of Nagasaki

Assorted Pearl Harbor Facts

51. Following the Pearl Harbor attack, many Americans began to distrust Japanese people living in the United States. 120,000 people with Japanese ancestry were imprisoned in special camps, even if they had US citizenship. Many people lost their homes and were separated from their families.

Japanese prisoners following Pearl Harbor

52. The Americans believed that Pearl Harbor was safe from torpedo attack because the waters of the naval base were too shallow for torpedoes to work properly. But the special torpedoes that the Japanese had developed worked well in shallow water and were able to cause immense damage.

53. Just after 7.00 a.m. on the day of the attack, two American soldiers were watching a radar screen which showed the Japanese airplanes approaching. As American bombers were due to arrive at Pearl Harbor that day, it was assumed that the radar was showing a group of American airplanes, and so no action was taken to defend against the Japanese attack.

54. The American bombers arrived at Pearl Harbor while the Japanese attack was taking place. They were unarmed, and so they couldn't shoot down any enemy planes - all they could do was try to land while being shot at by the Japanese. Luckily, all the American pilots survived, although one of the bombers was hit by the Japanese and split in two as it landed.

The split bomber after landing

55. The Japanese had a spy in the Hawaiian Islands who kept an eye on the movements of the US fleet. During the week, most of the ships were out at sea and came back to base at the weekend. It was decided to launch the attack on a Sunday because it was the only day of the week when nearly all the US fleet was anchored at Pearl Harbor.

56. Nearly half of the men who lost their lives at Pearl Harbor died on the *Arizona*. The ship still lies at the bottom of Pearl Harbor, and is now a war memorial. 1.5 million people visit the memorial every year to honor the 1,177 men who were killed when the Japanese bombs hit.

The Arizona Memorial

Illustration Attributions

The Japanese aircraft carrier, "Agaki"
Japanese military [Public domain]

A Japanese pilot with his scarf
PD-JAPAN-oldphoto

The Mitsubishi A6M
Kaboldy
https://de.wikipedia.org/wiki/Datei:Mitsubishi
_A6M_Zero_drawing.svg

The Aichi D3A
Kaboldy
https://pl.wikipedia.org/wiki/Plik:Aichi_D3A1_
Val.svg

The Nakajima B5N
Kaboldy
https://pl.m.wikipedia.org/wiki/Plik:Nakajima_
Kate.svg

Japanese planes preparing to take off
www.goodfreephotos.com

The "California" before the attack
OS2 John Bouvia, USN [Public domain]

The American aircraft carrier, "Yorktown"
U.S. Navy photo 19-N-17424 [Public domain]

American bombers at the Battle of Midway
Scouting Squadron 8 (VS-8), U.S. Navy; The original uploader was Palm dogg at English Wikipedia., 2006-01-30 (first version); 2006-02-14 (last version) [Public domain]

The bombing of Hiroshima
509th Operations Group [Public domain]

The bombing of Nagasaki
Charles Levy [Public domain]

Japanese prisoners following Pearl Harbor
US Department of Justice [Public domain]

The split bomber after landing
U.S. Navy [Public domain]

Made in United States
North Haven, CT
20 May 2025

69037524R00017